100% UNOFFICIAL

THE ULTIMATE GUIDE TO FRIENDS

First published in Great Britain in 2019 by Dean,
an imprint of Egmont UK Limited,
The Yellow Building, 1 Nicholas Road, London W11 4AN

www.egmont.co.uk

Written by Malcolm Mackenzie
Designed by Ian Pollard

ISBN 978 1 4052 9596 3

70756/002
Printed in Italy

Egmont takes its responsibility to the planet and its inhabitants very
seriously. We aim to use papers from well-managed forests run by
responsible suppliers.

100% **UNOFFICIAL**

THE ULTIMATE GUIDE TO FRIENDS

MALCOLM MACKENZIE

CONTENTS

Lifelong 'friends' on-screen and off.

FRIENDS IS THERE FOR YOOOU

● **It was recently voted the best sitcom ever* and who's going to argue with that? Um, probably Ross!**

Friends **helped make coffee shops 'a thing'. Starbucks opened its first UK café in 1998.**

The first *Friends* episode aired on 22 September 1994 to little fanfare. Nobody could've imagined then, that this sitcom about six New Yorkers in their twenties was about to become the TV phenomenon of the nineties, let alone foresee the impact it would have on popular culture and the enduring love it would continue to enjoy a quarter of a century later.

Friends is bigger than ever. It is one of the most seen TV shows in the world, and new generations of viewers are discovering it on streaming services every day. It's the perfect companion – when you need cheering up, when you want a cosy night in, when you fancy something playing in the background: *Friends*

*Ranker.com

When it comes to funny, the *Friends* cup sure runneth over.

The Ross and Rachel storyline was the backbone of the show.

is there for you. *Friends* is, as the title suggests, your ultimate TV friend.

Like all friends, *Friends* is imperfectly perfect. It doesn't get everything right, it's dated, and some jokes can seem a little 'off', (Joey! Joey! Joey!), but it is so freaking good that you can forgive it. *Friends* evokes a simpler time, when the internet and mobile technology didn't rule our lives, when trolling was done face to face – by Chandler, where hair wasn't dip-dyed lilac, but multi-layered and choppy. Clothes were huge, so were the apartments, and the hearts.

The success of *Friends* is down to three things: firstly the writing, which was consistently hilarious and moving. Never had an audience invested so much in the happiness of characters in a comedy. The second is those characters. What a brilliant mix: funny, weird, inappropriate, obsessive – each of the gang was a facet of a whole – like the Pixar movie *Inside Out*. Third is the casting. Those six actors were the dream team – no wonder

they have spent their entire careers trying to convince the world that they aren't actually Rachel, Phoebe, Ross, Chandler, Monica and Joey. They did their jobs well, almost too well, and all we can say is: clap-clap-clap-clap!

THANK YOU FOR

The stars reminisce about the greatest sitcom of all time.

'I don't know if I'd say it was my absolute favourite episode, but I loved doing *The One With the Blackout*. That was a memorable one, but there are so many.'
David Schwimmer

'It was my job to make people believe that I was that person. It's unconscionable to me to want to remove myself from *Friends*. It gave me every single opportunity. I appreciate it every single day, I promise.'
Lisa Kudrow

'I have this recurring nightmare – I'm not kidding about this. When I'm asleep, I have this nightmare that we do *Friends* again and nobody cares. So if anybody asks me, I'm gonna say 'no' [to a remake]. The thing is: we ended on such a high. We can't beat it. Why would we go and do it again?'
Matthew Perry

BEING A FRIEND

'That was lightning in a bottle to have those writers, those creators and the team they put together and the actors. It just worked, the casting was perfect, it really was.'

Courteney Cox

'It's a blessing and a curse. It gave us everything but also gives you more of a challenge, to shape people's perceptions of you. It's hard for people to even believe that we're playing other people.'

Jennifer Aniston

'We'll [Matt and his daughter] stop and watch it if we're channel surfing and it pops up. She loves to ask me questions about it. She'll say: "Was that real? Did you really eat that? What did that taste like? Ooh, you ate that off the floor? That's gross! You're so funny, Dad." It's fun to sit and watch it with her. She used to call it The Joey Tribbiani Show – but now she knows to call it *Friends*.'

Matt LeBlanc

SEASON 1

● **The one where we meet the 'friends' and slowly but surely fall in love, much like Ross and Rachel.**

We rank this **8th** best season

The gang watch Ben in his crib. Not exactly *The Avengers* in the excitement stakes.

MEMORABLE MOMENT

When Ross introduces everyone to his newborn son Ben, it's one of the most heart-warming moments of the season. After all of the bickering, worrying and competitive shenanigans with Susan, comes the joy of fatherhood. Not that it lasts by the way. What happened to Ben – huh? Justice for Ben!

IN A NUTSHELL

Chandler is not gay, which comes as a surprise to his colleagues ★ **Phoebe** finds a thumb in a fizzy drink and is awarded $7000 ★ **Rachel** gets a job at Central Perk, but does not get a job at Sak's Fifth Avenue ★ **Ross** becomes a father for the first time ★ **Monica** is a victim of identity fraud ★ **Joey** is Al Pacino's butt double and he stinks

Well it's not diet NOW.

Rachel's hair ...

has been backcombed and pulled through fourteen hedges.

At the beginning of the series, *Friends* was the 20th most watched show, but by the end it was the 2nd most popular show in America.

ENTER ... JUDY GELLER

Monica's mum and dad are fab supporting characters, but Judy Geller is a particular treat, delivering withering put downs to poor Monica at the most inappropriate moments, such as at the funeral of their grandmother when she tells her daughter to consider anti-ageing cream.

Crazy in love

On the list of 'who not to kiss', your best friend's mother has to be up there. But when Ms Nora Bing, international romance novelist, strokes Ross's ego by telling him he's the hero of his story and that Paolo is a mere secondary character, how can he not snog her. It's only polite, right?

THE AWARD GOES TO ...

Everyone! The gang picked up the People's Choice Award for fave new TV comedy series.

THE WISDOM OF JOEY

'When you're dead, you're dead, you're gone, you're worm food.'

11

THE ONE ...
Where Monica Gets a Roommate

Our fave episode from season 1

SEASON 1 PILOT EPISODE

● **So much of the show we know and love is set up in the very first episode!**

The gang scrutinise the first of many of Monica's BFs.

Funniest moment

Monica spitting in the face of Paul the Wine Guy is a solid LOL, but the consistency of Chandler's sarcasm even at this early stage wins the day – for example, when everyone goes bananas over Monica's new boyf, repeating his name over and over, Chandler drawls: 'I'm sorry, I didn't catch your name – Paul was it?' Classic Chan man.

Paul The Wine Guy deserved far worse tbh.

WHAT'S THE STORY?

Ross is crushed that his wife has left him for another woman, so when Rachel bursts into Central Perk in a wedding dress it's a sign. Because Rachel doesn't want to become Mrs Potato Head she moves in with Monica and gets a job as a waitress despite never having lifted a finger in her life. Meanwhile Monica's date is a lying toe-rag, Joey and Chandler can't put up shelves and Phoebe's a total weirdo – start as you mean to go on, right?

ICONIC LINE

'Oh I wish I could, but I don't want to.'
Phoebe

Here comes the bride all dressed in sopping wet white.

Style notes

Monica's strangely narrow braces and high-waisted slacks win the pilot stylespiration award, but in terms of classic fashion moments Rachel buying a new pair of boots when she has no job and no money lets us know straight away that Rachel is both stylish and a teeny bit spoiled. As for that wedding dress: I.C.O.N.I.C.

#FEELS

Friends is one of the first sitcoms to make you really care about the characters. When Ross wonders what woman he'd ever ask out and the screen fades to Rachel sat on her sadsome lonesome, it tugs on our hearts, but when he says that he just grabbed a spoon it gives actual goosebumps. Dead – and there are still 235 episodes to go.

This dissolve says so much about what's to come.

DID YOU NOTICE?

1
The cups at Central Perk are either empty or super sparing on the coffee.

2
Like Ariana Grande, Phoebe loves to riff on *My Favourite Things*.

3
Joey can often be found perching on furniture like an ungainly toucan.

CHANDLER

● **The king of sweater vests is sarcastic, self-deprecating and artfully mocking – and that's before breakfast.**

COULD HE BE ANY FUNNIER?

'Oh, no ... my diamond shoes are too tight.'

Diamond shoezone

Choosing between Julie and Rachel was hard for Ross, but Chandler had little, or rather no, sympathy for the man with two potential partners, letting rip in an escalating tirade of wit.

'Gum would be perfection.'

Trapped in an ATM vestibule with model Jill Goodacre, Chandler goes to pieces, but does he want a piece of chewing gum?

'Gum would be perfection.'

'Could have said, 'Gum would be nice'.

'But no, no, no. For me gum is perfection.'

Off the cuff!

When Chandler ends up handcuffed in Rachel's boss's office, (just another Tuesday), watching him squirm and try to use the phone with his nose is a hoot. Rachel isn't laughing though. Work LOLS, amirite?

The chase

Chandler was responsible for the most expertly choreographed physical comedy scene in all of *Friends*. When he spots Kathy on the street (S04, E05) it sparks a slapstick chase to rival Mr Bean, just so he can casually say hi.

EATS GARBAGE

CAUGHT IN DOGS

TAXI SCRAMBLE

SOOOO BREEZY

Bo peep and weep

Rachel is asked to wear the worst bridesmaid's outfit in the history of ever, giving Chandler the opportunity to give one of his greatest burns. It takes a second to get the joke, but that's what makes it so good.

'I'm sorry, we don't have your sheep.'

MEET MATTHEW

The youngest 'friend', **MATTHEW PERRY** has starred in a ton of stuff: from critically acclaimed series like *The West Wing*, *Studio 60 on The Sunset Strip* and *The Good Wife* to guest roles on fellow co-star's shows like *Cougar Town* (Cox) and *Web Therapy* (Kudrow). But the absolute peak of his career surely has to be *17 Again*, a body swap movie with Zac Efron. ZAC EFRON!!! Who wouldn't want to swap bodies with Zefron? *Faints*

SECRETS

Stuff every fan needs to know they know, y'know?

FROM THE SOFA

JENNIFER ANISTON didn't just dislike her famous Rachel 'do', she loathed it, going so far as to say, 'I think it was the ugliest haircut I've ever seen'. Um, bit harsh, Jen.

The only time one of the 'friends' broke the fourth wall and addressed the audience directly in character, was when Joey recapped the end of season three at the start of season four.

Joey's sandy but handy synopsis thing.

EARLY COUPLE MUDDLE

In the beginning, the show creators saw the central characters as Monica, Rachel, Ross and Joey. Phoebe and Chandler were only supposed to be supporting characters – Janices and Gunthers, if you will.

Every episode includes the word 'FRIENDS'.

Originally Joey and Monica were going to be the 'Ross and Rachel' of the show, but in a weird twist of fate, they are the only 'friends' never to actually kiss.

A band this cool should actually be called The Picassos.

The theme to *Friends* by **THE REMBRANDTS** was actually co-written by producers Marta Kauffman and David Crane. Wow, that's attention to detail.

Actor **JAMES MICHAEL TYLER** got the role of Gunther because he knew how to work an espresso machine. Wow, skills you never knew you needed as an actor.

THE SITCOM SITUATION

MATTHEW PERRY pitched a show about a group of friends called *Maxwell's House* to the TV network NBC, but they turned it down because they were already working on a similar show called *Friends* – what a coincidence!

COURTENEY COX was the only cast member not to be nominated for an Emmy Award for her work on *Friends*. Poor Harmonica!

LISA KUDROW was the only cast member never to have met any of the other actors before.

READY, SET, GO!

Where the action happens is almost as important as the action itself.

CENTRAL PERK

Central Perk was based on a real place called 'Arnold's Turtle', a veggie restaurant, but the whole feel was supposed to evoke the bohemian vibe of Greenwich Village coffee shops in the '50s and '60s, not Starbucks.

The paintings change every three episodes.

Sofa so good

The orange couch wasn't bought specially or custom made – no, this essential piece of furniture was found tattered and ripped in the corner of a basement at Warner Bros, just sitting there waiting for its big break.

ARTY PARTY

Artist Burton Morris created many of the pop art artworks that appear on the walls at Central Perk, but Gunther isn't his only fan – his paintings have been bought by Kanye West and Barack Obama.

MONICA'S

There was a hole in the poster behind Monica's TV so the crew could film through it.

Set designer Greg Grande described Monica's apartment as 'a whole new kind of eclectic taste with a flea-market, whimsical, and anything-goes style.' So now you know.

Good mauve

According to production designer John Shaffner, Monica's apartment was purple to help give the show its own identity. In theory you could be flicking channels, see Monica's apartment and instantly know where you are.

FREEZE FRAME

The iconic picture frame around Monica's peephole was originally a mirror, but the glass broke. Mind blown! A crew member smashed it by accident and they thought it looked cool so kept it.

Beam me up!

Sometimes there was an extra beam from wall to ceiling between the kitchen and lounge area. It became an inside joke, specifically added to every episode directed by James Burrows.

The fridge wasn't a dead prop. It actually worked and the cast and crew kept drinks in it.

SEASON 2

● **The one where they took some risks and messed with everything that they set up in the first season.**

We rank this

7th

best season

It's not his fault guys, OK? Smelly Cat makes his pop music debut. Cute and catchy.

MEMORABLE MOMENT

Everyone remembers where they were the first time they saw the music video to Smelly Cat – in front of their TV. Phoebe signs a record deal and stuns everyone, audience included, by the high production values, smoke machines, backing singers and um, Phoebe's rather TOO incredible voice.

ENTER ... DRAKE RAMORAY

Joey finally got his big break playing renowned brain surgeon Dr Drake Ramoray on daytime soap *Days of Our Lives* – making his first appearance in the 11th episode of season two. Sadly the fame doesn't last and Dr Ramoray falls down an elevator shaft, leaving him in a coma. His legacy of 'Smell the fart' acting will never die.

Rachel's hair ...

is a pouffy, layered choppy bowl-cut not unlike Gail from Coronation Street.

From this season onwards, all episodes are filmed on stage 24 on the Warner Bros lot. When the show finished it was named 'the *Friends* stage'.

IN A NUTSHELL

Phoebe is possessed by the spirit of Mrs Adleman ★ **Joey** moves out and **Chandler** gets a new roomie, **Eddie**, who doesn't like *Baywatch* but does like watching him sleep ★ **Monica** cannot save the fortunes of Mockolate ★ **Rachel** confesses her love for **Ross** and kisses **Ross** who dumps **Julie**, who throws things that hit **Ross**

THE AWARD GOES TO ...

The entire cast picked up best performance by an ensemble in a comedy series at the Screen Actors Guild Awards.

Crazy in love

If Rachel can't date Ross, by gum she's going to go for the next best thing, which is funny because he happens to be a doctor of gums: Russ. Russ is basically Ross with added chin and mullet. Monica puts it succinctly: 'They're as different as night and ... later that night.'

THE WISDOM OF JOEY

'Women love guys who love babies – it's that whole sensitive thing.'

THE ONE ...
Where Ross Finds Out

Our fave episode from season 2

SEASON 2 EPISODE 7

● *Friends* **is a funny show, but suddenly we're not laughing any more!**

We waited 31 episodes for this: 'smooooch'.

WHAT'S THE STORY?

This episode is all about Ross getting a cat, but not really. Rachel, fixated on the fact that Ross and Julie are planning on getting a cat, has 'one too many' and decides she needs closure. She begs a stranger to use his phone in a brilliantly funny date scene gone awry and leaves a message on Ross's answering machine telling him that she's over him. When he hears the message, the whole word implodes.

Funniest moment

The biggest LOLS come from the sub-plot where Monica relentlessly tries to whip a despondent Chandler into shape, giving us great lines like, 'She's got me doing butt clenches at my desk. And now, they won't bring me mail any more,' and visual gags like Chandler in lycra shorts and ducking out of jogging to get a cab instead.

When a taxi is also a getaway (from Monica) car.

ICONIC LINE

'I am the energy train and you are on board. Whoo-whoo.'

Monica

'Oh my god. Oh my god, Ross no, hang up the phone. Gimme the phone Ross, gimme the phone, gimme the phone.' And we're officially dead.

#GULP

David Schwimmer and Jennifer Aniston are so incredible in the scene where Ross finds out that Rachel used to 'like' him, that we feel ALL the emotions at once. Rachel is mortified that her secret is out and Ross is crushed when he realises what might have been, but he can't think straight: Julie is waiting for him and his brain glitches until all he can say is 'CAT'.

STYLE NOTES

Rachel's red check PJ bottoms were a sleepwear inspo for a generation, but when Phoebe appeared in Central Perk dressed/ upholstered like the actual *Friends* sofa complete with oversized buttons, it was troubling – since when did Pheebs want to blend into the background?

Orange you glad you matched your cardie to the couch?

WHAT DID WE LEARN?

1
Monica and Ross had a cat called Fluffy Miaowington.

2
Chandler defo fancies Monica. We get hints even at this early stage.

3
Without a remote, Joey will watch anything on TV– ANYTHING.

FRIENDS IN

What's the most interesting fact about *Friends*? Let's figure it out!

41/100
The score a test audience gave *Friends* in 1994

The ages of the cast at the start of the show

25
Jennifer Aniston and Matthew Perry

27
David Schwimmer and Matt LeBlanc

30
Courteney Cox

31
Lisa Kudrow

148
The number of episodes Gunther was in. That's more than Janice, Emily, Carol, Susan, Mike, Richard, Estelle, Jack and Judy Geller's appearances – combined!

236
The number of *Friends* episodes in total

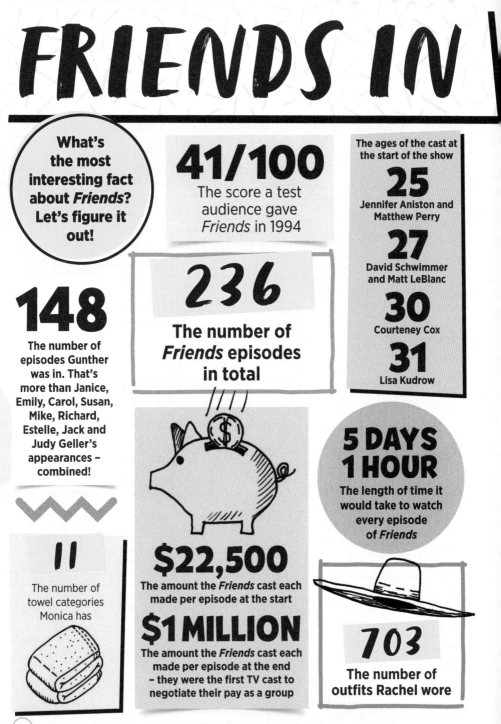

5 DAYS 1 HOUR
The length of time it would take to watch every episode of *Friends*

11
The number of towel categories Monica has

$22,500
The amount the *Friends* cast each made per episode at the start

$1 MILLION
The amount the *Friends* cast each made per episode at the end – they were the first TV cast to negotiate their pay as a group

703
The number of outfits Rachel wore

NUMBERS

5639
Joey's pin number – spells Joey

1,154
The number of cups of coffee drunk over the series by the cast. At 227, Phoebe drank the most!

100th
For the milestone 100th episode Phoebe gives birth to triplets

6
The number of Phoebe's dolls houses they had to make for a season three episode, because they had to set it on fire – and y'know, retakes

47.7%
The percentage of scenes Joey appears in – more than any other character

327
Thanksgiving takes place on the 327th day of the year. It crops up on the Magna Doodle in season 5 ep 8. There is a special Thanksgiving episode in every season except season two

9000+
The number of lines both Ross and Rachel had in the entire series – more than any of the other characters

1 MISSISSIPPI 2 MISSISSIPPI
How Ross counts

4 AM
The time at which they shot the opening credit sequence of the gang in the fountain

RACHEL

● **All the 'friends' had a funny quirk, (controlling, simple, sarcastic, kooky and dorky) except Rachel: Rachel was all of us!**

10 WAYS SHE IS ALL OF US

1 She overreacts …
When Phoebe tells Rachel there might be a spark between her sister Jill and Ross, Rachel goes totally overboard, barely able to breathe at the thought of their inevitable marriage. It's perfectly natural to catastrophise everything, because what if it's all true?

2 She's a romantic …
The fact she keeps going back to Ross tells us this, but even without Dr Dinosaur she's pretty gooey. When an attractive man leaves his phone in Central Perk, she imagines a romance blossoming between them both. I mean, he had Barney's department store on speed dial, what more proof could there be?

3 She's a dreamer …
Rachel uses a bottle of shampoo to pretend she's won a Grammy Award, making up a fake acceptance speech. We all do it – shocked face!

4 She's emotional …
She cries at the mere mention of the word 'wedding', and frankly who can't relate? Adverts, dogs with limps, Tuesdays – anything can set us off.

5 She can't cook …
She put beef in a trifle, but before you judge, what's the deal with mince pies? They don't have mince in, do they? Or do they? See, confusing isn't it? Blame the Tudors.

When mobile phones looked like baby monitors.

Tag is picture perfect.

Rach builds up her immune system.

6 She gets obsessed with guys ...

This follows on from the last few points. When she falls for a guy, she's very much the smitten kitten. After interviewing Tag for the role of assistant, her feedback was not 'efficient' or 'resourceful' but, 'I love him. He's so pretty I want to cry.'

8 She becomes irrational where good food is concerned ...

She ate cheesecake off the floor. Yum.

9 She likes to be entertained, not bored to death ...

She chose *Vogue* over *Wuthering Heights*: same. And her response to watching the *Discovery Channel*: 'Did you know that something really boring happened to someone really ugly in the Middle Ages?'

10 She loves her shows ...

Rachel is a massive fan of the soap opera *Days of Our Lives*. We also enjoy the occasional television programme – peas in a pod, really we are.

The bald and the beautiful.

7 She sometimes goes too far ...

Rachel can lose all perspective when put in a challenging situation, such as an ex turning up with a beautiful girlfriend. Bonnie wanted to be bald, OK? And as the saying goes: 'the course of true love never did run smooth' – unlike a head slathered in Veet.

MEET JENNIFER

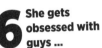

Rachel Green is played by **JENNIFER ANISTON**, who was the last to be cast and has arguably been the most successful since. Aniston has made a ton of great films, (*Dumplin'* and *Marley and Me*,) been on more magazine covers than Joey can count, is globally adored, and in 2018 was the third highest paid actress in Hollywood. In late 2019 she'll star with Reese Witherspoon, (who played her sister Jill in *Friends*) in a new show called *The Morning Show*.

ZOO YORK

● *Friends* could get pretty wild at times. Say hello to the most iconic furry and fine-feathered supporting stars.

Why wouldn't Chandler and Joey have farmyard animals in their apartment? Well, they're much easier to keep than a monkey – although Lisa Kudrow was a wee bit scared of Duck.

CHICK AND DUCK

MARCEL

Ross's bezzie Marcel was played by a pair of Capuchins, Katie and Monkey. They were cute, but shooting with them was very time consuming and they were ultimately written out. Since *Friends*, Katie has worked with Ariana Grande on *Sam & Cat*, and modelled with Kendall Jenner. Bananas, right?

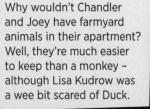

You can't argue with a feeling, so when Phoebe decides a stray cat is in fact her dead mum, who's going to argue? Well, Ross is, because Ross is a bit like that. Pheeb's mum is actually a little girl's cat, Julio.

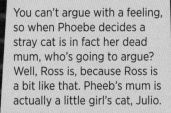

PHOEBE'S MOTHER

When you're sad, dogs cure everything with their wagging and such, but in a twist of events, Joey's pining over Rachel turns 'the happiest dog in the world' into one dejected doggy.

MUTTZARELLA

MRS WHISKERSON

When Rachel came home with a bald cat, it was hard to fathom what she or the writers were thinking. It was little more than a sight gag to mock the poor creature that Gunther thought was some kind of snake. Hisss.

PIGEON

Rachel is on the phone telling her mum that New York is cool and not to worry about her safety, before screaming and hanging up. Why? A pigeon flew through the window. She deftly captures it in a saucepan – free range dinner?

PAOLO'S CAT

Ross hates Rachel's boyfriend Paolo, but his ginger cat is just as bad. Ross is on the balcony having an intimate chat with Rach when the moggy launches itself onto him, causing much pain and laughter.

SEASON 3

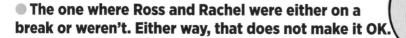

● The one where Ross and Rachel were either on a break or weren't. Either way, that does not make it OK.

We rank this
4th
best season

Something's getting Joey down and it's not just Chandler's constant mockery.

MEMORABLE MOMENT

It's been twelve years since Monica broke Ross's nose in the sixth annual Geller Cup and with so much water and cartilage under the bridge, the gang decide to play a 'friendly' game of football. First they 'bunny up' to choose teams and they're instantly at each other's throats. Eventually the girls win– hurrah – except they don't or maybe they do – who wants a Troll doll nailed to a bit of wood anyway?

IN A NUTSHELL

Rachel gets a dream job at Bloomingdales ★ **Monica** starts dating a cage fighter ★ **Joey** and **Chandler** adopt a chick and a duck – perfectly acceptable behaviour ★ **Ross** cheats on **Rachel** on 'a break' – totally unacceptable ★ Everyone can totally see up **Phoebe**'s boyfriend's shorts – not that they're looking or anything

Rachel's hair ...

is delicious with a cup of coffee, whipped cream and sprinkle of demerera.

Phoebe uses the word BFF – in 1997!!! Did the term actually originate here? If not, she sure did help to popularise its usage.

ENTER ... PHOEBE'S MUM

Phoebe wants to find her dad Frank, so with a little investigating she finds a family friend, also called Phoebe, who might be able to help. Eventually we find out why: Phoebe is Phoebe's mother!! How can we be sure? Well when she says she 'feels all floopy', it's a dead giveaway.

Crazy in love

When it comes to affairs of the heart Chandler doesn't have the best of luck, so hooking up with Joey's sister Mary Angela was always going to be a terrible idea. But it does make for a farcical fun time. Joey's seven sassy sisters should have had their own sitcom.

THE AWARD GOES TO ...

If being nominated is all that matters, then Lisa Kudrow must've been proud, as the only cast member to be nominated for an Emmy award.

THE WISDOM OF JOEY

'The Netherlands is this make-believe place where Peter Pan and Tinkerbell come from.'

THE ONE ...
Where No One's Ready

Our fave episode from season 3

SEASON 3 EPISODE 2

● **Will the gang be dressed in time for Ross's big night at the museum?**

Rachel punishes Ross, but will she make him drink that glass of fat?

Funniest moment

Monica isn't one to let things go, so when she hears a phone message from ex-boyfriend Richard that may or may not be old, she has to respond. She calls and leaves her own message, which she assures everyone is breezy. In a moment of rare intelligence, Joey informs Monica that saying you're breezy 'negates' all breeziness.

Space is breezier than Monica.

WHAT'S THE STORY?

Ross has invited everyone to a black tie benefit at the museum, but everyone is far too distracted to get dressed, much to the annoyance of Ross. Chandler and Joey are taking bickering to Olympic levels of pettiness, Monica is obsessing over Richard, Phoebe is covered in houmus, and Rachel suddenly thinks she might stay home and catch up on some correspondence. This is one of the purest episodes ever: six friends, one room – boom!

ICONIC LINE

'It was a casual, breezy message. It was breezy.'

Monica

'Look at me. I'm Chandler, could I BE wearing any more clothes?'

Bottled magic

The One Where No One's Ready is the first of many 'bottle episodes' – that is, an episode that takes place on a pre-existing set without guest stars, to keep costs down. Bottle episodes get their name from *Star Trek*, who created 'ship in a bottle episodes' set entirely on the *Enterprise*. Far from seeming second-rate, these episodes are beloved by fans because they pack in more jokes and quality time with our favourite characters without the plot getting in the way.

SQUABBLE TROUBLE

If this episode is about anything, and it really isn't, it's about the love Joey and Chandler have for winding each other up. Chandler wants 'his' chair back, but Joey won't give it up, so for some reason Chandler steals all his underwear, forcing Joey to do the 'exact opposite' by wearing all his clothes at once – without any underwear, of course. Mature.

Chandler gets comfy on Joey.

DID YOU KNOW?

1 This special episode was the 50th episode of *Friends*.

2 This was the only *Friends* episode to take place in 'real time'.

3 Jay-Z recreates this episode with a black cast for his *Moonlight* video.

DO YOU SPEAK FRIENDS?

Friends totally changed the way we speak, dude!

Top 10 Friends phrases

These Friendisms are still used everywhere: from Yemen to the Pennsylvania Dutch.

1 'Oh-My-Gawwd ...'
Janice – So simple – in EVERY season!

2 'Friend Zone'
Joey – Somewhere you never want to visit.

3 'Going Commando'
Joey – not wearing underwear, not OK.

4 'We were on a break'
Ross – the excuse of weak-willed idiots.

5 'He's her lobster'
Phoebe – Have you found yours yet?

6 'How You doin'?'
Joey – It's used in Camila Cabello's 'Havana'!

7 'Meat sweats'
Joey – The reason Quorn was invented.

8 'I'm Breezy ...'
Monica – Yup, nuthin' to see here.

9 'Could I 'Be' any more ...'
Chandler – This stress pattern is rife in life.

10 'Smell the fart acting'
Joey – Just try watching Holby City now.

IN THE 'NO'

Are you a Rachel, Monica or Phoebe?

'Noooo'
– Rachel

'I KNOW'
– Monica

'Oh No!'
– Phoebe

You couldn't make it up!

Friends binned the dictionary and invented its own language. Here are the best 10 words.

 1 Unagi
Definition: Being ready for anything.

 2 Frenaissance
Definition: When you rekindle an ailing friendship.

 3 Transponster
Definition: Chandler's job, probably.

 4 Gleba
Definition: Emma's first word.

 5 Koondis
Definition: The thing removed from Ross's bum by Guru Saj.

 6 Whoopah
Definition: The sound of a whip cracking.

 7 Mississippilessly
Definition: Counting without putting Mississippi between the numbers.

 8 Oomchimawa
Definition: What you say after a kiss.

 9 Scrud
Definition: A not very nice person.

10 Nubbin
Definition: A third nipple.

MEME PHEEB

Phoebe has more quotable lines for the modern age than any other 'friend'.

'My eyes!'
USE: Any time you see something horrible.

'That is brand new information.'
USE: Whenever someone tells you something you already knew.

'I can't, because I don't want to.'
USE: If you really can't be bothered.

'MONICA'

A contender for most used *Friend*-word is an actual 'friend' themselves. We now use the word Monica to describe being uptight and overly clean, e.g.:

'Put down the broom and stop being such a Monica, Karen.'

JOEY

● **Joey Tribbiani: actor, model, fashion maverick, wearer of hats. Forget Rachel, Joey is the real sitcom style star.**

7 MEMORABLE LOOKS

CHIC AHOY

Whether you're yachting up the Hudson or simply lounging on your LA-Z-Boy chair, 'Nautical' is an evergreen staple you can rely on.

PORSCHE FOR THOUGHT

When you don't have the car, dress in clothes inspired by the car – that's how the mini skirt caught on.

HOLY COWBOY!

How the west was NOT won – in silky white satin.

DO I A'MOOSE YOU?

DO NOT TRUST THIS DOCTOR

Not what Joey's hairdresser meant when he suggested a little mousse in his hair.

Despite playing Dr Drake Ramoray, Joey is not a trained neurosurgeon, or indeed a trained anything.

A LITTLE ELF HERE

ROMAN KNOWS

'Hello *Vogue*, if you think gladiator sandals are cool, wait till you see THIS!'

Santa's most adorable lil' helper is not Bart Simpson's dog, but Joey 'stripy britches' Tribbiani.

MEET MATT

Like Courteney Cox, **MATT LEBLANC** started out as a model and his Heinz ketchup ad was super famous in the 80s. Before *Friends*, he appeared on sitcom *Married With Children*, playing Vinnie Verducci, who was even more Italian than Joey Tribbiani, if you can believe it. After *Friends*, he starred in the spin-off show *Joey*, *Episodes* and *Top Gear*, plus he made some movies including *Lost In Space* with his old pal Gary Oldman.

SEASON 4

● **The one where Ross gets married, and Chandler and Monica finally become more than 'friends'.**

We rank this

3rd

best season

If only dock leaves grew at the beach.

MEMORABLE MOMENT

One of the most iconic moments in *Friends* history takes place off screen. When Monica is stung by a jellyfish, she hops up and down screaming and there's only one way to alleviate the pain according to Joey – pee on the sting. Does it work? We never find out, wee-ly.

ENTER ... EMILY

Keep the boos down at the back! Ross's girlfriend Emily couldn't help not being Rachel, any more than Julie or Bonnie could. She was annoying so we were thrilled when it ended, but it was fun for British audiences to see the show go to the UK for their wedding which featured a brilliant turn by Jennifer Saunders, sweetie darling.

Rachel's hair ...

is long, and layered with a hairslide like an almost edgy five year-old.

Rach is ready for her nightie out with the in-laws.

A close-up of Rachel's wedding invitation from Ross shows her name spelled Rachel Greene. He really should have known better – tsk.

IN A NUTSHELL

Phoebe decides to become a surrogate mother for her brother **Frank Jr** ★ **Joey** uses Charlton Heston's shower ★ **Rachel** wears underwear to dinner because it's a real dress (if she says it is) ★ **Chandler** and **Monica** get together in the shock twist of the whole show ★ **Ross** meets, falls in love with, proposes to, and marries **Emily**

Crazy in love

Monica was obsessed with Richard, so of course she fell for his son, a fitter, younger version of his dad. Rachel is disapproving: 'it's like inviting a Greek tragedy over for dinner.' Phoebe thinks 'it's twisted', and Joey is all, 'Eww-eww-eww'. In Monica's defence, he was pretty fit.

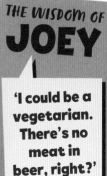

THE AWARD GOES TO ...

Lisa finally wins the outstanding supporting Actress in a Comedy series award at the Primetime Emmy's. Yay Pheebs.

THE WISDOM OF JOEY

'I could be a vegetarian. There's no meat in beer, right?'

39

THE ONE ...
With the Embryos

Our fave episode from season 4

SEASON 4 EPISODE 12

● **Phoebe gives the greatest gift ever and the gang put their friendship to the test.**

Yay – group hug.

#Feels

It's possible to read Phoebe as a one-dimensional oddball, but episodes like this really flesh out the person behind the whimsy. Lisa Kudrow digs deep and finds heart in her storyline, and whether she's singing to the potential embryos or bracing herself to take a pregnancy test, we're behind her 100% with a lump in our throats and a tear in our eye.

Phoebe discovers she's pregnant.

WHAT'S THE STORY?

Chandler and Joey think they know more about Monica and Rachel than the girls know about them, so with the help of quizmaster Ross they put their money and their sanity where their mouths are, in an epic battle of wits with ever-increasing stakes. Meanwhile, Phoebe goes to the hospital to become the surrogate mother for her half-brother Frank Jr and his wife Alice. The procedure is an expensive one-time deal, but JOY, Phoebe gets pregnant.

ICONIC LINE

'My sister is going to have my baby.'

Frank

Monica's competitive streak sees the girls lose their apartment to the boys.

Testing times

Friends fans should sit with a pad and pen during this episode because so much background info is spilled in Ross's ridiculous test of knowledge. Joey's imaginary friend was called Maurice, Rachel's favourite movie is *Weekend At Bernie's*, Monica's pet peeve is animals dressed as humans and the name on Chandler's *TV Guide* subscription is Miss Chanandler Bong.

GAME CHANGER

The tables finally turn.

After four seasons, *Friends* was ready for a big shake-up and the boys switching apartments with the girls was almost as big a shock as Phoebe carrying a baby for her brother. Rachel couldn't believe it was happening and neither could we, but as Joey said, 'You can't just ignore the bet, it's a bet. You bet in a bet. If you lose, you lose the bet.' Quite simple.

WE ALSO LEARN

1 Monica got a pencil stuck in her ear when she was 14.

2 Michael Flatley, Lord of The Dance, scares the bejesus out of Chandler.

3 Joey's all time favourite food is sandwiches.

TOP 10

BEST OTHER HALVES

The 'friends' kissed a lot of frogs before finding true love. Here are the best other halves, ranked for your consideration!

1

JANICE

'Oh my goodness!' No, that's not right. 'Oh my gosh!' Nope, nearly there. 'OH-MY-GAWWD!' There she is, the number one bundle of shrill brilliance: Janice Litman. How did Chandler ever let her go? Legit ledge!

2

MIKE

If *Friends* was a game, Phoebe won – because Mike. Sorry Ross, but Mike is our lobster. Not only is he funny, he's rich and cute and, unlike nearly everyone on this show, not at all annoying – plus he slays invisible piano. Here's to Crap Bag.

3

Was there ever a cuter co-star? The answer is no. When Rachel first met her assistant she thought he was a model and took a Polaroid – we used the pause button. Tag didn't have a last name, y'know, like Rihanna, Adele and Cher, but more adorbs.

TAG

4

CAROL

Ross's first wife, who left him for another woman, is actually someone we like, unlike, say, Emily, but picturing them together is quite hard. She seems fairly grown up and normal. Maybe that was the problem and she tired of his boyish ways.

5

JULIE

Yes he was a terrible person who grabbed Phoebe's bum, but he was also a necessary obstacle and early source of joy because Ross hated him so much. The Italian hunk didn't speak good English, but he did look good in '90s knitwear.

6

PAOLO

Timing is everything and poor Julie couldn't have arrived in Ross's life at a worse time. In fact she was so ruddy nice that we felt terrible for wanting her relationship with Ross to fall apart. Hopefully she met a nice man, like ... Richard.

7

RICHARD

Tom Selleck was an '80s heart-throb when he appeared in *Friends*, but despite an age gap you could drive a bus through, Monica and Richard had more chemistry than any other couple on *Friends*. HEAT!

8

CHARLIE

Charlie brought some much-needed diversity into the friendship group, and she had loads going for her, so much so that both Joey and Ross fell head-over-heels. But she arrived too late and was ultimately a mere distraction. Shame.

10

DUNCAN

Chandler and Joey compete over everything, but when Chandler fell in love with Joey's girlfriend Kathy, things got complicated. Kathy was cool, a bit too cool for the 'friends', and definitely worth living a day in a box for.

9

KATHY

They didn't go out, but the shock twist of season one was that Phoebe was married – to a gay ice dancer. It turns out he's actually straight and needs a divorce to marry the woman he loves, which is sadly not Pheebs. Dat costume doe!

FRIENDS IN

There's magic in small things – props to the props!

PAT THE DOG
Joey bought him with his *Days of Our Lives* money and from then on he was a looming presence. (Also 'pat the dog' – geddit?)

1

2

THE GELLER CUP
A Troll doll nailed to a bit of wood that means more to Monica and Ross than dinosaurs and detergent.

3

GLADYS AND GLYNNIS
These creepy, three dimensional paintings by Phoebe will haunt us forever. So very terrifying.

4

CHICKEN SOUP FOR THE SOUL
The book that made Chandler cry is a great self-help book, but *Be Your Own Windkeeper* has a lot more LOLS.

9 OBJECTS

5

SHELL LAMP & DOLL CLOCK
When Mr Heckles died he left the girls some really exquisite pieces. Monica was especially thrilled!

6

MOCKOLATE
We weirdly want to taste this fake chocco treat just to see how foul it really is.

HUGSY
Nap time is nothing without Joey's bedtime penguin pal Hugsy, although Ross Geller comes a close second.

7

8

MAGNA DOODLE
The ever-changing gizmo hanging on Chandler and Joey's door was like the secret subtext of the show with its cryptic (and not so cryptic) messages.

9

APOTHECARY TABLE
We're more into IKEA, but there's no denying Pottery Barn do a great apothecary table.

45

PHOEBE

● **A journey into Phoebe's most wackadoo moments from just a little bit silly to totally batty cray-cray.**

HOW CRAY IS SHE?

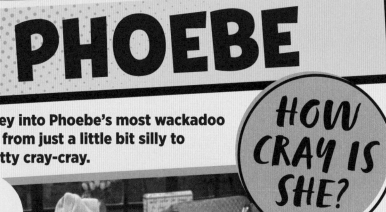

KNIT TWIT

Even getting dressed isn't simple for Phoebe. She's waiting for a telephone call to be answered when she decides to put on a polo-neck jumper and gets her head trapped in the sleeve, yelling, 'Monica, I'm scared!' Shoulda stuck to sweater-vests like Chandler.
Cray rating ❗❗❗

SANTA SHOCKA

Discussing the possibility of selfless acts, Joey mentions Santa Claus, and then the fact that he doesn't exist and Phoebe's brain explodes behind her eyes.
Cray rating ❗❗

MS PAC IT IN

Buying a giant retro arcade game, Ms Pac-Man, for Monica and Chandler is pretty nutty, but when Phoebe loses she lets out an unholy tirade of swear words.
Cray rating ❗

PRINCESS CONSUELA

After marrying Mike, instead of changing her name to Mrs Hannigan, Phoebe decides to be creative and settles on the new moniker (not Monica) Princess Consuela Banana Hammock.
Cray rating !!!!!

CHORD BLIMEY!

Phoebe doesn't know the names for musical chords so she names them after the shapes her hand makes such as bear claw, turkey leg and old lady.
Cray rating !!!!!

GOING FOR COLD

When Phoebe got a cold her voice sounded so gravelly and cool that when she got well, she licked Monica's fluey cup to get ill again.
Cray rating !!!!!

REGINA PHALANGE

Phoebe regularly uses the fake name Regina Phalange. Sometimes she's a medical doctor, a French make-up representative or simply a businesswoman in town on business.
Cray rating !!!!!

MEET LISA

LISA KUDROW famously almost got the part of Roz on sitcom *Frasier*, but was replaced at the last minute. Thank goodness, because Lisa IS Phoebe. Well actually she's not, she's a brilliant award-winning actress starring in hilarious films and TV shows like *Romy and Michelle's High School Reunion*: classic, and *The Comeback*: genius. Lisa is one of many comedians (Kristen Wiig, Maya Rudolph) who started in LA's The Groundlings comedy school.

47

SEASON 5

We rank this **the best season ever!**

● The one where everything is perfect, the cast are all on top form and the stories are hilarious and emosh.

Who could've predicted that Ross and Rachel would get married? No one! Brilliant.

MEMORABLE MOMENT

Vegas baby. When Chandler and Monica's one year anniversary is hijacked, everyone tags along making it the best holiday ever, because this time Phoebe's there, not like that London fiasco. Joey finds his hand twin, Phoebe is plagued by a lurker and Monica and Chandler decide to get married on the roll of a dice but – holy twist-a-rama – when they get to the wedding chapel, a sozzled Ross and Rachel are stumbling out having just tied the knot. Jaws. To. The. Floor.

IN A NUTSHELL

Phoebe gives birth to triplets ★ **Ross** splits up with **Emily** ★ **Chandler** and **Monica** become a thing to rival the thing that **Rachel** and **Ross** can't give up ★ **Joey** gets a man-bag ★ **Rachel** is savaged by her bald cat ★ Everyone makes a bunch of resolutions they can't keep – oh, but they can keep a ball in the air for ages. #skills

Rachel's hair ...

is sleek, conditioned, honeyed and roguishly drawn on with a Sharpie.

Episodes like *The One Where Phoebe Hates PBS* opened British eyes to the world of our American cousins. PBS is a TV channel a bit like the BBC.

ENTER ... THE YETI

Rummaging around in the storage facility surrounded by creepy dolls is giving Rachel (but not Monica) the heebies, so when a wild hairy yeti man emerges from the dark wielding an axe, the girls freak out and smoke bomb the creature. Rachel puts her 'big foot' in it, then dates him.

Crazy in love

Joey's girlfriend Katie is a big hit with everyone. Unfortunately for Joey she's a big hit for him – right in the arm. Katie won't stop thumping Joey in the name of exuberant jest, and it's all fun and games until Rachel finds herself on the receiving end of a wallop. Big mistake.

★ THE AWARD GOES TO ...

The show, for best comedy at the first Teen Choice Awards. Lisa Kudrow is nominated for a SAG Award.

THE WISDOM OF JOEY

'It is odd how a woman's purse looks so good on me, a man!'

THE ONE ...
Where Everyone Finds Out

Our fave episode from season 5

SEASON 5 EPISODE 14

- **Monica and Chandler go public, but not before the ultimate game of *Dare*!**

'My eyes, MY EYES!' Rachel and Phoebe see Chandler and Monica.

Enter Hugsy the penguin

Joey hates lying about Monica and Chandler, because keeping secrets is hard, plus he tells Rach and Pheebs, 'I've got secrets of my own, y'know?'. He then confesses to sleeping with a cuddly toy: Hugsy his bedtime penguin pal. We think this is a throwaway line, but a couple of scenes later Joey is seen taking a nap with a certain Hugsy.

Happy Sleep. Joey and Hugsy 4EVA.

WHAT'S THE STORY?

When Ugly Naked Guy moves out of his flat, Ross decides he wants it and books a viewing. Phoebe and Rachel tag along for a snoop, but get much more than they bargained for when they look out the window and see Chandler and Monica smooching. Instead of confronting them about it, *Inception* levels of confusion ensue with each group of friends calling each other's bluff. Meanwhile Ross ends up butt nekkid at Ugly Naked Guy's house.

ICONIC LINE

'They don't know that we know they know we know.'

Phoebe

Pretending to fancy your best friend: could there BE anything more cringey? Ewwwww.

Funniest moment

Witness the least sexy seduction in the whole of TV history, but possibly the funniest. Phoebe knows Chandler's dating Monica but she isn't supposed to know, so in the ultimate game of 'chicken' she messes with him by coming on strong. But he knows her game and plays along. Who will be the first to crack? 'Here it comes, our first kiss,' Phoebe announces, before the pair lock lips like two reluctant turtles after a long dry summer.

#FEELS

This episode illustrates why *Friends* is regularly the number one show on Netflix. One second we can barely breathe with laughter as Chandler and Phoebe fake kiss, and the next we're fighting back tears of joy as Chandler makes his declaration of love, 'I'm in love with Monica. I love her. I love her. I love you, Monica.' Oof! So darn good.

And so Mondler was born, or is it Chanica?

WHAT DID WE LEARN?

1
Ugly Naked Guy has broken ... moonboots, a trampoline, and um, a cat.

2
Doing the laundry seems to be a national pastime in America.

3
Phoebe puts on perfume by walking into a spritz of mist.

MORE

SECRETS

FROM THE SOFA

There's a lot of gossip under those cushions, y'know.

The laughs are real!!! *Friends* was filmed in front of a live studio audience of about 300 people. Shooting an episode usually took five to six hours, with 20 minute breaks between scenes.

The audience made so much noise when '80s hottie **TOM SELLECK** was on set that some scenes had to be re-filmed with no audience.

ALL SET FOR CENTRAL PERK

You know what's on the other side of Monica and Rachel's lounge walls? It's not Monica's bedroom, it's the set to Central Perk. They only re-built the bedroom sets when they needed them.

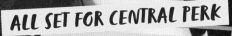

first assistant director   Ben Weiss
second assistant director   Carlos Piñero

There are a couple of times you can see *Friends'* actors genuinely laughing. One is in episode 22 of season four when Joey sneezes/laughs. You can also see Rachel controlling her sniggers as the credits roll while Ross plays the bagpipes to Phoebe's shrill screams in episode 15 of season seven.

You can see what the actor who voices Homer Simpson looks like in episode 12 of season two. **DAN CASTELLANETA** plays the zoo janitor.

Joey famously plays fictitious Dr Drake Ramoray in *Days Of Our Lives*. Well, *Days Of Our Lives* is a **real** American soap opera and in **real** life **JENNIFER ANISTON**'s dad is an actor who has played Victor Kiriakis in it since 1985.

Producers and writers hang out on the sofa for a cute in-joke.

Newcomers to *Friends* might not realise that the sitcom had a spin-off TV show. *Joey* ran for two seasons, giving us 46 Tribbiani-packed episodes. DAVID SCHWIMMER directed two of them.

Like *The Simpsons*, *Friends* has its very own 'sofa gag'. At the start of episode one of season three they walk into Central Perk to find the couch occupied – by none other than executive producers **KAUFFMAN, BRIGHT AND CRANE**.

BEST CELEB GUESTS

● *Friends* had more A-list guest stars than cappuccinos. Some were well known, some just starting out: here's our favourite ten!

1

BRAD PITT
AS WILL COLBERT

Brad Pitt was, and still is, one of the biggest actors in the world. Luckily he was a good sport and hilariously mocked his real life love for Jennifer Aniston by playing someone who loathed her so much he started a club.

2

JENNIFER COOLIDGE
AS AMANDA BUFFAMONTEEZI

Ahh-mahn-dah is one of the loopiest and funniest *Friends* characters of all time, but did you know, the *Legally Blonde* actress and star of Ariana Grande's *Thank U, Next* video, also played Joey's agent Bobbie Morganstern in 46 episodes of the spin-off *Joey*?

Stranger Things happen than two girls kissing at college, but whereas for Rachel it was a bit of fun, for Melissa, played by Ryder, it meant a whole lot more. Movie stars never used to appear on TV, but shows like *Friends* helped to change that.

3

WINONA RYDER
AS MELISSA WARBURTON

4

COLE SPROUSE
AS BEN GELLER

It's hard to believe that in another life *Riverdale*'s Jughead Jones is a Geller, but actor Cole Sprouse played Ross and Carol's very sweet son Ben from season 6-8. Then Ben mysteriously vanished – perhaps it had something do with Hiram Lodge.

5

BRUCE WILLIS
AS PAUL STEVENS

Julia Roberts started the trend for partners of cast members appearing in guest spots. Matthew Perry was dating her when she popped up as a girl from school who Chandler humiliated. As Susie, Roberts is cruel, cunning and charming.

6

JULIA ROBERTS
AS SUSIE MOSS

Dating one of your students is never a great idea, Ross, especially when her father is Bruce Willis. Willis plays it so cool and natural that when he finally ramps up the ridiculous, it's completely unexpected, and hysterical.

7

ELLEN POMPEO
AS MISSY GOLDBERG

Before Doctor Meredith Grey, there was Missy, the hot girl with the side pony from Ross and Chandler's past, whose anatomy they both agreed to steer clear of. Sadly Chandler lied and was regularly tasting Missy's chapstick.

8

GEORGE CLOONEY
AS DR MITCHELL

When George Clooney appeared in *Friends* he was famous for playing a doctor on the TV show ER, so getting him to play an MD with co-star Noah Wyle was inspired. Watching Monica and Rachel scare the dream-boats off was SO HARD.

10

JENNIFER SAUNDERS
AS ANDREA WALTHAM

When Joey meets fellow actor Richard Crosby, played by Gary Oldman (aka Sirius Black), he tells him that he's just won an Oscar, which as a viewer today is freaky, because back in 2001 he hadn't won one, but now he has.

9

GARY OLDMAN
AS RICHARD CROSBY

The British comedy ledge plays the posho step-mother of Emily who's permanently answering her mobile with pouffy hair and clown amounts of blusher. She's one of the high points of the scenes filmed in London.

SEASON 6

● **The one with a few guest stars that don't exactly add much to the beef trifle, but y'know – ratings!**

We rank this **5th** best season

> No one ever looks as ridiculous as Ross, except for Monica. Together, they are pure toe-curling excellence.

MEMORABLE MOMENT

Monica is competitive about everything, and that extends to dancing. When they get tickets to *Dick Clark's New Year's Rockin Eve*, Ross suggests they crack out the old 'routine', which Monica reveals has not been attempted since they were kids. Forget *Dirty Dancing* – witness this car crash and you're guaranteed to have the time of your life.

IN A NUTSHELL

Joey learns to knit ★ **Chandler** can't cry ★ **Rachel** gets a job at Ralph Lauren and **Phoebe** thinks she snogged him, but it was just **Kenny**, the copy guy ★ **Ross** whitens his teeth and icebergs are jealous of their purity ★ **Richard** tells **Monica** he still loves her and she has to choose between him and **Chandler**. Spoiler: she chooses **Chandler**

> The teeth maketh the man.

Rachel's hair ...

is looooong like a pony's tail, but it's not in a pony tail, it's loose and swishing free.

We think of *Friends* as being a '90's sitcom, but this was the last series to take place in the 1990s. Ross and Monica famously celebrated the year 2000 (left).

ENTER ... RACHEL'S SISTER JILL

Legally Blonde star Resse Witherspoon appeared in two episodes as Rachel's ditzy little sister who, like Rachel in the first episode, finds herself being 'cut off' by their dad – this time for buying a boat for a friend. Reese plays the spoiled brat with glee, making Rachel seem grounded.

Crazy in love

After much soul searching and temptation from men with moustaches, Monica takes matters into her own hands, fills the apartment with more candles than a church at Christmas and proposes to Chandler. When she can barely get the words out through the tears, he proposes back and suddenly we're the one with weepy eyes.

★ THE AWARD GOES TO ...

Bruce Willis won an Emmy for his portrayal of the father of one of Ross's students – who Ross is dating.

THE WISDOM OF JOEY

'When I had health insurance I could catch on fire, you know or get hit by a bus. Now I gotta be careful!'

THE ONE …
With Unagi

Our fave episode from season 6

SEASON 6
EPISODE 17

● **Ross messes with the wrong women and gets a face full of floor wax.**

Chandler makes Monica the most beautiful Flaffanfaffler.

It's a twin thing

Joey's running low on headshots and needs money fast so his first (actually his only) thought is to offer his body up to science. Sadly science isn't interested. The only medical study taking place is for twins, so Joey thinks he's beaten, then he thinks again and hires fellow actor Carl to play his twin. They look nothing alike, but hey, it worked for Drake Ramoray.

Joey's terrible twin, Carl.

WHAT'S THE STORY?

Phoebe and Rachel have been taking self defence classes but Ross, who studied 'Ka-ra-té', is concerned that they're complacent and need to be aware of DANGER at all times, explaining the ancient Japanese concept of 'Unagi'. Rachel points out that Unagi is sushi and Phoebe backs her up, much to Ross's annoyance. Meanwhile Chandler and Monica have to make Valentine's gifts with varying success and Joey seeks medical assistance.

ICONIC LINE

'Unagi is a state of total awareness.'

Ross

Rach and Pheebs try out some new yoga moves.

Funniest moment

When Ross hides in the hallway and jumps out at Phoebe and Rachel shouting 'Danger!!', they don't take it lying down – oh no, that's something they've got planned for sensei Ross. Breaking into his apartment, they lurk behind the curtains waiting to pounce and take down their prey. Taking him down and squashing his face into the floor, the master hilariously becomes more of a disaster.

SOFA SWAP

Just before the credits at the end of the episode, Rachel and Phoebe are forced into the window seat because – SHOCK HORROR – the sofa is taken. This is one of only three times this happens in the series. In this instance it serves the story, giving the girls a front row seat to Ross attacking another pair of girls he thinks are Rachel and Phoebe.

Doesn't it look weird to see strangers on the sofa?

GET THIS ...

1
The word Ross is looking for is actually 'Zanshin'. Unagi really is an eel.

2
Monica's closet has wire hangers in it. Surely she'd have something fancier.

3
The Way You Look Tonight on Chandler's tape is sung by Tony Bennett.

ROSS

● Ross was the smartest 'friend' and also one of the funniest, but despite life's obstacles his spirit was never crushed.

AT HIS MOST ADORKABLE

SANTA IS CANCELLED!

When Ross can't find a Santa costume for Christmas, does he quit? No, he grabs the next best thing – an armadillo suit – giving son Ben and Monica an unforgettable Hanukkah.

DOCTOR TWO TAGS

PROFESS-AURUS

Only Ariana Grande and tinnitus can equal the high pitched noise that Ross makes when impersonating a velociraptor for his students.

Sometimes, thoughtful Ross can come across as patronising Ross, like the time he wore two name tags just to be, y'know, clear.

OH RUGGER!

LEATHER AIN'T CLEVER

As resolutions go, wearing leather trousers seems easy. Until you pull them down, can't get them back on and the lotion and talc form a paste.

He might come across as a softie, but Ross has grit, like the time he suffered all manner of scrapes during a rugby match to impress Emily. If only she'd liked croquet!

PIVOT

When manoeuvring a sofa up stairs you only need shout one word, 'Pivot', over and over again. Everyone will understand what you mean, 'PIVOT! PIV-AT!' Try it.

MEET DAVID

DAVID SCHWIMMER was bitten by the acting bug when he saw Ian (Gandalf) McKellen perform Shakespeare and never looked back. After appearances on *Blossom* and *NYPD Blue*, he got his big break on *Friends*, but after the show finished he never stopped working, taking on more serious roles in TV shows like the acclaimed *Band of Brothers* and playing Kim Kardashian's dad in the award-winning *American Crime Story*.

SHUT IT, YOU OLD BAG

Ross goes above and beyond to learn the bagpipes for his sister's wedding, with hilarious consequences.

UNFORGETTABLE
FASHION

Friends fashion was as awful as it was great. Who can forget these style choices?

TEENY

X When Ross takes back Rachel's fave tee, he says he'll wear it all the time. God we hope he was lying!

FRANKIE SAY RELAY

SOCKS

X ✓ Early Joey was very pretty, especially when he came home all dolled up from his work as an actor/model/butt double.

GLOWING

✓ Rachel had a bunch of cute outfits, but with this check mini skirt and sock moment she wasn't monkeying around.

ELEGANT

BOSOMS

X Monica looked pretty bad when Phoebe cut her hair, but she looked way worse in her '50s diner get up where melons were always on the menu.

✓ Phoebe usually looks like a psychic's tablecloth, except for when she wore this lovely green tea dress. Flawless.

CASUAL

✓ Chandler's waistcoats were awful, as were his boxy mafia shirts. This graphic T-shirt was a rare glimpse of normal.

CLUBBED

X Gunther's garish style choices were never worse than this magician's assistant situation.

CRINKLED

X For some reason Carol and Susan decided to get married as a pair of Ferrero Rochers.

SEASON 7

We rank this **6th** best season

● Let's be honest, it's all about Chandler and Monica's wedding, which is great: bridezilla Monica is LOLS.

Phoebe and Ross had a friendship we couldn't get enough of.

MEMORABLE MOMENT

Each of the friends has a special relationship, but this season Ross and Phoebe stole the crown for most aww-some 'friends'. When Ross discovers that Phoebe can't ride a bike because she never had one, Ross buys Pheebs her dream bike and teaches her how to ride it. Sure beats being pulled around on a box.

ENTER ... CECILIA MONROE

... The *Days of Our Lives* soap diva with slaps for days and a hair-trigger drink-throwing reflex, played brilliantly by Susan Sarandon. She plays the formidable Jessica Lockhart who meets a tragic end and has her brain transplanted into the body of Dr Drake Ramoray. Hooray, science!

Rachel's hair ...

Say hello to bob.
'Hi bob, how you doin'?'
At this point in the show
Rachel's hair is the
7th friend.

David Schwimmer
directed four
episodes in season
seven, so basically
– he was NEVER on
a break.

IN A NUTSHELL

Phoebe's fire alarm won't stop beeping ★ **Joey** is nominated for a Soapie Award (the third most prestigous soap award) ★ One of **Ross's** male students is in love with him, but not really ★ **Monica** and **Chandler** get married and **Rachel** steals **Monica**'s wedding thunder when we find out that she's pregnant

★ THE AWARD GOES TO ...

Jennifer Aniston wins the People's Choice Award for fave TV performer, and both Jen and Lisa Kudrow are nominated for Emmys.

Crazy in love

Everyone has the hots for Ross and Monica's cousin Cassie, including actual relation Ross, who feels terrible about it, but not so terrible that he doesn't lurch in for a kiss. Cassie's secret weapon, apart from her face, smile and everything, is her amazing glossy hair. Pantene/10.

THE WISDOM OF JOEY

'You will be
scored on a
scale of one
to ten, one
being the
highest.'

THE ONE ...

With Phoebe's Cookies

Our fave episode from season 7

SEASON 7
EPISODE 3

● **This episode really takes the biscuit and leaves Joey and Rachel all out at sea.**

Ross tests batch number 17 – whoops – or is it 16?

WHAT'S THE STORY?

Chandler and Monica are gratefully receiving engagement presents and Phoebe reluctantly offers up her grandmother's famous cookie recipe. Unfortunately the recipe was lost in a fire and Joey eats the last cookie, which turns Monica into a baking fiend as the gang try to figure out the ingredients. When Phoebe recalls the story of her great grandmother, Nestlé Toulouse, it becomes clear that the beloved recipe came from a supermarket packet of biscuits.

Funniest moment

When Chandler announces that he's wearing glasses at the start of the show, little do we expect the storyline to go where it does, namely into the lap of his future father in-law. 'Why do they put so much steam in there?' cries Chandler later, cringing at the faux pas. 'Otherwise they would have to call it the 'room room', offers Ross. Classic.

Chandler should've got contacts.

ICONIC LINE

'I'm not yelling at you, I'm just yelling near you.'

Rachel

Rachel tries to get through to Joey: 'Do you want to pay attention or do you want to die?'

Ahoy there, Ms Meanie!

It's no surprise that spoiled Rachel was given a boat by her father as a child. 'He was trying to cheer me up, my pony was sick,' she reveals with no hint of irony. When she offers to teach Joey the ropes, literally, they enter choppy waters straight away, with Rachel barking orders like a gruff sea dog. Joey is not a fan of 'mean Rachel' and neither is Rachel who realises that somehow she's turned into her dad.

STYLE NOTES

Fashion comes in cycles, and the twenty year rule is a pretty good one. This episode was first aired in the year 2000 but the casual fashions seen in this sofa hangout could be from now. Stonewashed jeans and baggy long-sleeved T-shirts are totally coming back into fashion. Chandler's thin rim specs, not so much.

On Fridays we wear stonewash.

WE NEED ANSWERS!

1 What was in the recipe to batch 16 that made Ross nearly throw up?

2 Was Monica trying to escape or eat a squirrel at fat camp?

3 Which side is port again? And what's a Cunningham and why has it got to be tight?

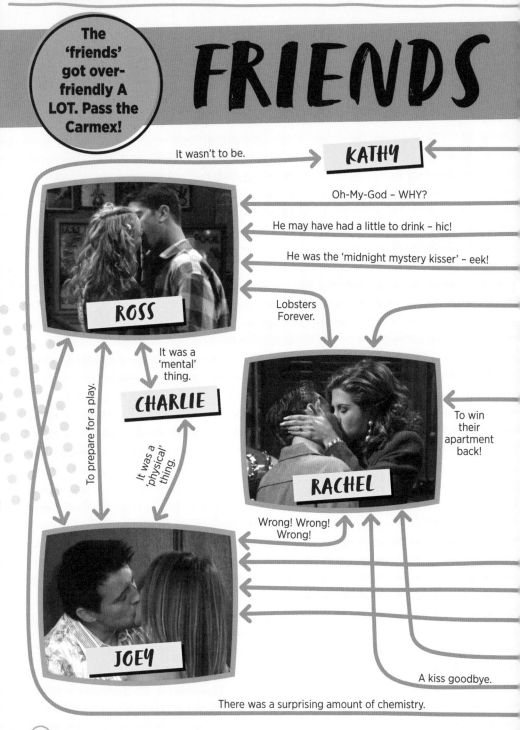

FRIENDS

The 'friends' got over-friendly A LOT. Pass the Carmex!

It wasn't to be. → **KATHY** ←

Oh-My-God – WHY?

He may have had a little to drink – hic!

He was the 'midnight mystery kisser' – eek!

ROSS

Lobsters Forever.

It was a 'mental' thing.

CHARLIE

It was a 'physical' thing.

To prepare for a play.

RACHEL

To win their apartment back!

Wrong! Wrong! Wrong!

JOEY

A kiss goodbye.

There was a surprising amount of chemistry.

KISSING TREE

They crossed the line!!!

JANICE

He was her Bing-A-Ling!

Flashback kisses x 2.

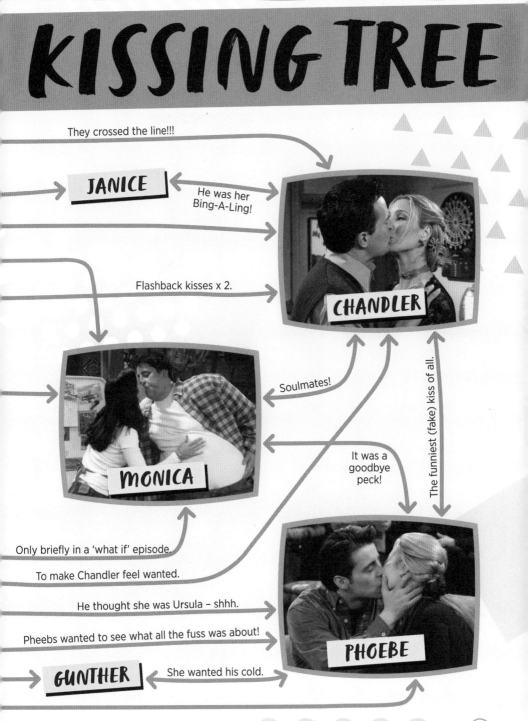

CHANDLER

Soulmates!

MONICA

It was a goodbye peck!

The funniest (fake) kiss of all.

Only briefly in a 'what if' episode.

To make Chandler feel wanted.

He thought she was Ursula – shhh.

Pheebs wanted to see what all the fuss was about!

GUNTHER She wanted his cold.

PHOEBE

FUNNIEST

There are so many unforgettable flashback funnies in *Friends*, but the best are ...

'80'S CHANDLER AND ROSS
From the Flock of Seagulls hair, Hall and Oates tash to the Miami Vice suits, hilarious fashion hi-jinks.

RACHEL'S 'REAL' NOSE
'They had to reduce it because of my deviated septum.' Yeah right Rach, we believe you.

MACARONI CARROT FINGER FLIRTING
Monica really did win the flashback episodes – she was *everything* doing the turkey fez dance, and then *this* happened!

FLASHBACKS

ARMLESS PHOEBE
In her past lives, Phoebe was a wartime nurse with a habit of losing arms. Stupid funny.

TURKEY-HEADED JOEY + MONICA
When someone tells you to get stuffed, this is not what they mean, Joey. As for Monica, well ...

MONICA DANCING
Flashback 'fat Monica' was not just a one-note visual gag, she was utterly adorable, and boy did she have the moves.

SEASON 8

● **A near perfect award-winning season celebrates the unmatchable chemistry of the six friends.**

We rank this **2nd** best season

HOPPING BONUS

HUNGRY MONKEY

LADDER OF CHANCE

THE WHEEL OF MAYHEM

THE WHEEL OF MAYHEM

TIME TURTLE

WICKED WANGO CARD

The boys are completely and utterly Bamboozled!

MEMORABLE MOMENT

The game show *Bamboozle* is the most tantalising 'What if?' ever. Joey has an audition to be the new host of a complex game show and tests out the script on Ross and Chandler. The rules are so bonkers and fun that it's a wonder no one made this TV show. Someone. Make. This.

ENTER ... EMMA

Ugh, here come the tears again, and not just Rachel's – sniff. After a long hard labour, baby Emma is finally born – named after her favourite Spice Girl, or possibly at Monica's suggestion – we don't know what goes on in their heads! She's adorable and so are Ross and Rach as utterly besotted parents. Why can't they just get back together?

Rachel's hair ...

looks great. It's the season with all the wins, choppy streaked shoulder-length joy.

Friends sure loved Eric Clapton: his songs play out the finale episodes of both season six and eight.

Sorry guys, Gunther wins as Charlie Brown.

IN A NUTSHELL

Toby is addicted to baths, sorry, **Chandler** ★ **Monica** has a secret closet ★ **Joey** proposes to **Phoebe** and **Rachel** – **Phoebe** says yes, but sadly nothing comes of it ★ The man in the red sweater is **Rachel**'s baby daddy ★ Halloween is a battle royale between Supergirl and Cat Woman, the Easter Bunny and a space potato

Crazy in love

Phoebe and Ursula may look alike, but inside Ursula's a rotten egg, so when her fiancé Eric (Sean Penn) finds out, he breaks up with her. Who better to comfort him than Phoebe, right? Wrong! Eric can't even look at Pheebs because of her face. Split-screen love triangles are hard.

THE AWARD GOES TO ...

Jennifer Aniston, who won her first Emmy for her run of pregnancy episodes, and *Friends* won their first and only Emmy for Best Comedy.

THE WISDOM OF JOEY

'Thanksgiving with no turkey is like Fourth of July with no apple pie! Or Friday with no two pizzas.'

THE ONE ...
With the Rumour

Our fave episode from season 8

SEASON 8
EPISODE 9

● **The biggest movie star on the planet makes the best TV show ever, even better!**

How many people you can cram around one side of a table?

WHAT'S THE STORY?

It's Thanksgiving and Monica has invited old school friend Will to join them for dinner. The only thing is, Will hates Rachel. Will, played by Aniston's then husband Brad Pitt, was an overweight geek at high school, and Rachel was something of a bully. At first she thinks Will, who she can't remember, is giving her flirtatious smouldering looks, but pretty soon it becomes clear his brooding stares are the squints of loathing. More yams, anyone?

Funniest moment

The laughs come thick and fast in this episode but Phoebe kills it with every utterance. First she fake screams at the TV, then she reveals she didn't go to high school, but learnt French behind a dumpster, then, when Will confesses that he started a rumour about Rachel, she yells what all of us were thinking, 'Come on, Will, just take off your shirt and tell us.'

Phoebe and Will, the romance we deserved.

ICONIC LINE

'Here come the meat sweats.'

Joey

The reunion of the 'I hate Rachel Green' club welcomes the guest of honour.

Rachel is the Pitts

Will Colbert does not just loathe Rachel, he co-founded the 'I hate Rachel Green' club, with none other than – dun, dun, dun – Ross. What makes this so funny is that at the time Jennifer Aniston and Brad Pitt were the most famous couple in the world – the Kim K and Kanye of their day, only more so. Getting them to spit insults at each other on screen was a masterful stroke of comedy genius, and it's the pits that this was Will's only episode.

I hate Rachel Green

STYLE NOTES

According to Joey, turkeys are ugly, stupid and delicious – also a Tribbiani is never full, so when Monica cooks an entire turkey just for Joey, he's certain he can finish it, but first he needs to change into his 'Thanksgiving pants', aka Phoebe's maternity trousers, also known as her melon-stealing slacks. Do keep up.

Joey prepares to face his 'Everest'.

WHAT DID WE LEARN?

1 Monica once had an imaginary boyfriend called Jared.

2 Ross dated the 50 year-old school librarian, Mrs Altman. R.I.P.

3 Fingers do *not* swell up to twice their size during pregancy and stay that way.

MONICA

● **Competitive, clean and a little bit mean, Monica Geller is the OG perfectionist queen.**

... IS A TOTAL 'MONICA'

CLEANLINESS CREATOR

Monica loves to clean and we see this from episode two when she buzzes around the room snatching a glass from Joey as he drinks from it and fluffing pillows that are quite fluffed enough. We later discover that she even cleans in her sleep.

PLATE PROTECTOR

Monica loves her wedding crockery like Joey loves pizza. To proect it, she goes as far as to suggest cutting food while you hold it so as not to cause any damage.

The first rule of being friends with Monica: do not engage in any competitive behaviour. Monica refuses to lose and takes no prisoners, clawing her way to victory.

GAMES COMPETITOR

THIEF INSINUATOR

SWITCH DETECTOR

Monica, as we've discovered, is not breezy – she is, in fact, fairly OCD. When she finds a useless switch in Joey's apartment she HAS to find its use, despite the cost. Poor Mrs Katrakis.

When Monica thinks the cleaner is stealing clothes from her, there's only one thing to be done – crawl between her legs to look for tell-tale wear and tear. This is not OK.

WEDDING DICTATOR

Planning Phoebe's wedding was a role Monica was up for – at least that's what the clip-board, headset and stringent use of military time suggest.

ILLNESS OBJECTOR

Unlike most of us, Monica refuses to acknowledge that she's ill, because sickness is weakness. Watching Mon try her best to be sexy while ravaged by a flu-like virus is, however gross, a proper giggle-splutter.

MEET COURTENEY

Before *Friends*, **COURTENEY COX** was most famous as the girl Bruce Springsteen picks out of the crowd in his video to *Dancing In The Dark*. She also co-starred in *Ace Ventura: Pet Detective* and appeared as one of *Seinfeld*'s many girlfriends. After the show, she starred in the *Scream* franchise as tenacious news reporter Gale Weathers and made six seasons of the successful sitcom *Cougar Town*. Grrrrr.

77

FRIENDS MYSTERIES SOLVED

REVEALED

After many years of speculation, in 2016 the actor who played Ugly Naked Guy was finally revealed by the *Huffington Post* to be Jon Haugen. And in the scene he had with Ross you'll be glad to know he was wearing boxers.

● **Questions will be answered, cans will be opened, worms will be everywhere!**

DECOYS R RUSS

Yes – David Schwimmer played Russ, Rachel's bizarrely familiar boyfriend in episode ten of season two. The cameo role was credited to a performer named Snaro, but we can confirm that Mr Snaro was Mr Schwimmer.

The one without the handclaps: in episode three of season one there is no handclap sound in the opening credits. It's the only one out of 236 where there is no clapping sound over the theme tune. Weird huh? Apparently there was nothing mysterious about this, and Warner Bros have explained the hiccup as a 'technical glitch associated with the master-cut' – m'kay.

CLAPLESS

Critics of *Friends* have often carped about the fact that the bezzies always get the couch at Central Perk, but in 2015 sleuths at Bustle discovered the answer to this decades-old mystery. There is sometimes a reserved sign on the table. It's not there very often, but it's fun to try and spot.

RESERVED

A WEE PROBLEM

Peeing on a jellyfish sting, as Chandler did for Monica, might actually make it more painful. Adding fresh water can cause more venom to be released and urine has pretty much the same effect as water. Vinegar can help though, so they shoulda gone straight to the chippy.

In 2017, 21 years later, Matt LeBlanc finally explained the real reason why he had a sling in season three episode three. In the episode, we're told that Joey fell off his bed, but in reality he got the injury in the previous episode where he dislocated his shoulder after jumping, and missing, a chair in a petty battle with Chandler.

'ARMFUL

POT'S GOING ON?

In 2018, *Buzzfeed* reported that the episode where the girls went to Pottery Barn was in fact low-key product placement, which according to a Warner Bros exec was necessary to 'offset the high cost of production'. After the story ran, Pottery Barn reached out to deny that they paid for the privilege. Hmmmm? Looks like this is one for Detective Mac Machiavelli.

SEASON 9

● Season 9 is a bit disappointing after season 8 which was such a Saturday. Season 9 isn't even a Thursday!

We rank this the least best season

Sibling rivalry between the Greens gets out out hand.

MEMORABLE MOMENT

The Thanksgiving episodes are always a high point and this is no different. The delicious side-order, served on Monica's best wedding crockery, comes in the shape of Amy: Rachel's sister (who isn't Reese Witherspoon) played with award-winning bite by Christina Applegate, who's so bad she's great!

IN A NUTSHELL

Phoebe gets a guest role on *Days of Our Lives* ★ **Chandler** gets a new job and feels old ★ **Monica**'s hair threatens to take over her entire body ★ **Joey** considers investing in an emu farm – which sounds like a way better idea than **Rachel** falling in love with **Joey** ★ In good news, **Phoebe** meets **Mike** and then **Mike**'s parents, WOAH!

Humidity + hair = frizz.

Rachel's hair ...

Oh baby cheeses! Rachel fell into a field of dip-dyed razor blades and became Avril Lavigne.

Season nine was originally going to be the last season of *Friends*.

ENTER ... CHARLIE

On paper you'd think palaeontology professor Charlie, with a history of dating Nobel prize winners, would be a dead match for Ross. She does end up with him, but not before a few trials and Tribbianis. Barbados changes everything – poor Joey just can't hang on to his GFs.

THE AWARD GOES TO ...
Jennifer Aniston wins the Golden Globe for Best Actress in a TV comedy, and the People's Choice Award for Favourite TV Performer.

Crazy in love

Supergirl dates Ant-Man – it's the comic book crossover no one saw coming. Seriously though, Paul Rudd is a brilliant addition to the show as Mike, the man Phoebe eventually marries. He pretty much became the bonus 'friend' in the final two seasons, appearing in 17 episodes.

THE WISDOM OF JOEY

'Name your first born child Joey! Someone has to carry on my family name.'

81

THE ONE ...
With the Blind Dates

Our fave episode from season 9

SEASON 9
EPISODE 14

● **Weirdo Steve from season 1 returns to date Rach, but she doesn't remember him!**

Phoebe reveals her diabolical 'plan laugh,' waa-ha-ha-ha!

WHAT'S THE STORY?

Phoebe and Joey set Rachel and Ross up on terrible dates in the hope they'll discover how good they are for each other and get back together. To mark the occasion, Phoebe unleashes her maniacal 'plan laugh' and desire to escape to Mexico – sorry – wrong plan. When Joey accidentally fixes Ross up with his perfect woman, they have to cancel, leaving Ross stood up and Rachel with Phoebe's most creepy client.

Not in front of the B.A.B.Y.

Emma is adorable and Chandler and Monica are happy to babysit, but they really want a baby of their own, so they sneak off to the bedroom while she's napping. Joey comes in and, horrified by the situation, takes Emma back to his apartment, which sends Chandler and Monica into a spiral of panic. Thankfully Joey did not feed Emma pizza.

Suddenly Joey has morals.

ICONIC LINE

'If you wrap up my free crab cakes, I'll be on my way.'

Ross

Rachel's 'worst date ever' draws to a close.

Funniest moment

Rachel's entire date is hysterical because Steve, played by actor Jon Lovitz, is the biggest loser to ever step into the lives of the friends, and that's saying something. By his own admission, he's neither handsome, rich nor funny, and is probably infertile but his funniest admission comes during the end credits, when sat alone he yelps, 'I have such fat hands'. Ridiculously, awkwardly brilliant.

WAITING GAME

Being stood up is the worst, so it adds insult to injury when a sassy waiter tells Ross that the staff of the restuarant are taking bets over

'Are you worried your date, came, saw you and left?'

how long he'll sit waiting. The waiter even offers Ross free food to get him to stay. It must have been good too, because Joey and Ross return for more crab crakes at the close of the show.

DID YOU NOTICE?

1 The Valentine's card saying 'Love' on the Central Perk table? This aired 6 Feb 2003.

2 When Joey and Phoebe are outside, you can clearly see fake snow dusting the street.

3 *Buffy The Vampire Slayer* guest stars (sorta), on the cover of *InStyle* at the newstand.

SECRETS

FROM THE SOFA

More gossip than the Post Office on Friday lunchtime. BOOM!

Ross's middle name is Eustace, Rachel's is Karen, Joey's is Francis and Chandler's is Muriel – laughs for a week. Like Ross, Monica's begins with an E, but that's all we have and Phoebe doesn't have a middle name – that we know of.

Is this Frank and Phoebe's first meeting?

A potato is once seen under the cake cloche. Was Gunther all for cutting down on sugar before it was trendy?

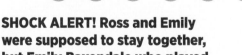

Spud muffin? The '90s were pretty weird.

The actress who plays Joey's agent Estelle, **JUNE GABLE**, also plays the nurse who delivers Ross's son Ben. Also the actor who plays Phoebe's brother Frank, **GIOVANNI RIBISI**, appeared in an earlier episode (season 2, ep 6) as a guy who tips Phoebe when she's about to busk outside Central Perk.

SHOCK ALERT! Ross and Emily were supposed to stay together, but Emily Baxendale who played Emily was pregnant and didn't want to keep filming in America. Thank heavens for that.

For some reason Chandler's sexuality had a question mark over it. LISA KUDROW assumed his character was gay after the first table read of the script, Chandler's co-workers think he's gay and MATTHEW PERRY appeared in an *SNL* sketch joking about it. Speculation was so rife that in 1996 co-creator DAVID CRANE confirmed that Chandler was not gay, OK?

Phoebe: the Taylor Swift of Central Perk.

FRIENDS INDEED

The cast did a little group hug before the start of filming every week.

LISA KUDROW hated playing the guitar so much she suggested Phoebe play the bongos instead. Lucky for us Kudrow was given lessons.

Friends NEVER filmed in New York. Not once. Ever.

In the opening credits of the first episode of season six, all the cast have the name **ARQUETTE** added to their name in honour of **COURTENEY COX**, who (much like Ross and Rachel in the previous episode) had recently tied the knot to Scream co-star **DAVID ARQUETTE**.

COURTENEY COX ARQUETTE
JENNIFER ANISTON ARQUETTE
LISA KUDROW ARQUETTE
MATTHEW PERRY ARQUETTE
MATT LE BLANC ARQUETTE
DAVID SCHWIMMER ARQUETTE

Friends had great beginnings. All but the Green sisters arrived in season one.

BEST ALMOST FRIENDS

● The absolute best *Friends* characters who are not featured in the credit sequence larking about with an umbrella.

1

URSULA

Weirdly, Phoebe's twin sister started life as a bit-part on a completely different show: *Mad About You*, before *Friends* even existed. Her brand of low-key evil is so much genius and easily the most fun recurring character.

2

GUNTHER

Poor unloved, overlooked Gunther. In an alternate universe, the manager of Central Perk's unrequited love for Rachel is the real story of *Friends*. The blond barista goes to extremes to be close to his one-time employee but it just isn't to be.

3

When we meet Joey's larger-than-life agent with her gravelly voice, lipstick teeth and carousel of cigarettes, it becomes clear why his career might not always go so well. She's basically an *SNL* sketch inserted into the show. Ridiculous fun.

ESTELLE

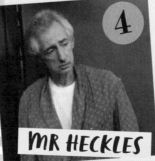

4

MR HECKLES

The weird old geezer from downstairs, who was perpetually disturbed by the awful noise from Monica and Rachel's flat, seemed like a pernickety busy body, but all he wanted was some peace for his non-existent cats and oboe practice.

Ross and Monica's parents are always a treat when they pop up. Jack Geller is such a dad with his oblivious witterings and bad jokes and Judy is pure middle class snobby snark. Her sole goal in life seems to be making Monica feel bad, which is not only a guilty pleasure, it sheds a whole lot of light on the Geller siblings' psyche.

JUDY AND JACK GELLER

JILL & AMY GREEN

Phoebe's not the only one with a troubling sister – Rachel's are next-level annoying. Amy is self-involved and mean and Jill is needy and whiny, and both are totally selfish. Because the 'friends' have to be likeable, it's up to family members to play the villains and Rachel's spoiled, petty siblings do that delightfully.

The girlfriend and eventual wife of Ross's ex Carol is the bomb. Susan is a refreshing palate cleanser, a feminist trailblazer that refuses to be bossed around by a man. Who can forget the time she made Ross pretend to give birth?

UGLY NAKED GUY

SUSAN BUNCH

Sure, Ugly Naked Guy was the butt (heh-heh) of many jokes, but he lived a full and pretty experimental life, what with his Thigh Master, hammock and gravity boots. He was house proud, into DIY, he dated and danced. At least he wasn't permanently glued to a PS4.

SEASON 10

● **The last couple of seasons weren't the best, but it was still hard to say goodbye. Now pass the tissues ...**

We rank this **9th** best season

How can one empty room cause so much sadness?

MEMORABLE MOMENT

Seeing the cast in Monica's empty apartment is like being stabbed repeatedly in the left phalange. When all the friends reveal they each have a key to the flat, it's another wrench, and the fact it looks like Jennifer Aniston, rather than Rachel, is fighting back tears, will finish anyone off – even Chandler.

IN A NUTSHELL

Charlie breaks up with **Ross** ★ **Rachel** and **Joey** try to mess with our minds (and eyes) ★ Despite the blizzard, **Phoebe** and **Mike**'s snowy wedding outside Central Perk is a romantic wonder ★ **Monica** and **Chandler**, who thought they couldn't have kids, do have kids, two of them, thanks to birth mother **Erica**, played by Anna Faris.

The first of many happy endings.

Rachel's hair ...

Oh hey, finger flickin' California girl. Was Rachel off to Paris or Malibu? Don't answer that.

In America, the last episode was the most watched TV show of the decade.

EXIT ... EVERYONE EXCEPT JOEY

When Joey and Chandler, the bestest buddies in all of TV, hug out their goodbyes after a lame cool guy handshake, we think we'll never see either of them again. We were only half wrong. Joey Tribbiani retuned to TV in his own sitcom *Joey*. No one from *Friends* appeared in it *sobs*.

Crazy in love

When Ross and Rachel get together in the penultimate episode, we think it's all over, but NO, Rachel bids the gang adieu. Ross chases her to the airport, but we're thwarted again and again. All looks lost, but then Rach turns up on Ross's doorstep and ... finally we can breathe.

★ THE AWARD GOES TO ...

Jennifer Aniston was once again the People's Choice and Teen Choice favourite. Jen A and Lisa K really were the gong girls of *Friends*.

THE WISDOM OF JOEY

'I am pretty wisdomous.'

In the last season Joey admits what we suspected all along.

89

THE ONE ...
With Ross's Tan

Our fave episode from season 10

SEASON 10
EPISODE 3

● **Season 10 was not one of the best, but this episode was a solid 10/10.**

Amanda comes between Monica and Phoebe.

Forever Friends

Rach and Joey ignore the instincts telling them NOT to get romantically involved and power through. 'Sexy, sexy,' Rachel says, lighting candles furiously. The sight of Joey and Rachel kissing is SO wrong that when they realise they're better off as friends it comes as sweet relief, and when they tell each other they love each other – well just try not to cry.

Rachel can't work out why it won't work out.

WHAT'S THE STORY?

Ross wants to get a bit of colour, Phoebe and Monica want to 'cut out' an annoying old friend, Rachel and Joey want to take their relationship to the next level and Chandler wants to ping Monica's bra with telekinesis: this episode really crams it in. Oh, and it's touch and go between Monica and Phoebe for a while when Monica discovers Phoebe tried to 'cut out' Monica in 1992. They make up with the best backhanded compliment ever.

ICONIC LINES

'I went to that tanning place your wife suggested.' **Ross**

'Was that place – the sun?' **Chandler**

Ross really should have counted Mississippi-lessly.

Funniest moment

Cackling while Ross fails at life is one of the great joys of *Friends*, and David Schwimmer has a gift for physical comedy that makes you want to see bad stuff happen to him – like accidentally getting a fake tan over and over and over again. He asked for a two and he got an eight. There's a life lesson in there somewhere: if life gives you eights, maybe stay at home and shower before you go back for more of the same.

AMANDA IS BETTER

She's had no dance training, you know?

How to make an obnoxious show-off hilarious: hire Jennifer Coolidge. Jennifer, last seen cameoing in Ariana Grande's 'Thank U, Next' video, is comedy gold as Ahh-mahn-dah, the girl from Yonkers with a fake British accent and a habit of announcing her exceptional qualities: 'Smell my neck, it's not perfume, its me'.

HOW TIMES CHANGE

1
The girls mention mobile phones repeatedly, but still use a landline – oh 2004.

2
There's so much bread and pastry at Monica's, which would so be carb-free today.

3
Rachel hasn't seen *Blue Planet*, or else she wouldn't be drinking from a plastic bottle.

THE TEST

● **Think you stan *Friends*? Take our fiendish *Friends* challenge and find out!**

1 **Which actor is Joey a butt double for?**
A ☐ Al Pacino
B ☐ Robert De Niro
C ☐ Tom Hanks

2 **Who was Chandler's roommate before Joey?**
A ☐ Chad
B ☐ Kip
C ☐ Brett

3 **What was Emma's first word?**
A ☐ Ball
B ☐ Ross
C ☐ Gleba

4 **Who was Monica hoping to look like when she let Phoebe cut her hair?**
A ☐ Eric Roberts
B ☐ Joan Collins
C ☐ Demi Moore

5 **Who did Monica actually end up looking like?**
A ☐ Phil Collins
B ☐ Dudley Moore
C ☐ Julia Roberts

6 **Which '80s popstar slapped Chandler?**
A ☐ Boy George
B ☐ George Michael
C ☐ George Benson

7 **What does Joey take to the hospital when Ben is about to be born?**
A ☐ A sandwich
B ☐ A beer
A ☐ A portable TV

8 **Rachel has a poster of what in her bedroom?**
A ☐ Audrey Hepburn
B ☐ Excelsior sewing machine
C ☐ Chanel No5 perfume bottle

9 **What street does Phoebe live on?**
A ☐ Bleecker Street
B ☐ Christopher Street
C ☐ Morton Street

10 **The character names in *Friends* are inspired by which US soap?**
A ☐ *Sunset Beach*
B ☐ *Dynasty*
C ☐ *All My Children*

11 **Monica's apartment number changed from 5 to what number?**
A ☐ 20
B ☐ 19
C ☐ 18

12 **What was Gunther's first word in the show?**
A ☐ Rachel
B ☐ Yeah
C ☐ Chandler

13 **How many brothers and sisters does Chandler have?**
A ☐ None
B ☐ One
C ☐ Three

14 **What was the name of the diner where Monica worked?**
A ☐ Happy Days
B ☐ Moondance
C ☐ Swing Time

15 **What caused the fire in Phoebe's apartment?**
A ☐ VCR machine
B ☐ Hair straighteners
C ☐ A gas leak

16 **What are the names of Monica and Chandler's twins?**
A ☐ Maisie and Jack
B ☐ Maisie and Noah
C ☐ Erica and Jack

17 **Which US state does Ross forget?**
A ☐ Delaware
B ☐ Colorado
C ☐ Maine

18 **In which month does Thanksgiving fall?**
A ☐ October
B ☐ November
C ☐ December

19 **How many hand claps are there in the opening credits?**
A ☐ Four
B ☐ Five
C ☐ Six

20 **Who turns the lamp off at the end of the opening credits?**
A ☐ Ross
B ☐ Rachel
C ☐ Monica

YOUR SCORE

1-7
Crap bag
Sure it's hard to remember stuff, like what Chandler does for a living, but you just Joey'd yourself to the bottom of the class. Watch more *Friends*.

8-13
Shoop! Shoop!
You're right in the middle, baby, like pastrami and cheese in Joey's sandwich. You 'heart' your *Friends* a lot, but you're not total besties. Yet.

14-20
Yay you.
The Geller cup is SO yours, dude. You Bamboozled your way to the finish and slayed. You're Monica in the best possible way: i.e. without the eyepatch, frizz and smell of Cif.

Answers 1-A, 2-B, 3-C, 4-C, 5-B, 6-B, 7-A, 8-B, 9-C, 10-C, 11-A, 12-B, 13-A, 14-B, 15-B, 16-C, 17-A, 18-B, 19-A, 20-C.

THE GELLER-GREEN-BING

It's 20 years since *Friends* hit its peak – we give the awards the cast truly deserved!

WINNER!

Courteney Cox

BEST SHOWCASE OF THE WORST OF US

Courteney was phenomenal as Monica, and possibly the most underrated *Friends* character. The way she takes our worst traits: nit-picking, competitive bully, and keeps it breezy is a magic trick even Ross couldn't master.

WINNER!

Matt LeBlanc

BEST ACTOR IN A STRAIGHT-JACKET OF MISOGYNY AND DUMBNESS

It's a testament to Matt's charisma and acting ability that he takes a drooling dimwit and makes us laugh with him, but when you realise he's basically a child in a man's body (30 going on 13?) suddenly it all makes sense.

WINNER!

Jennifer Aniston

BEST FRIEND

Jennifer Aniston somehow took the character of a spoiled rich girl and turned her into the 'friend' we'd want to be friends with (and steal the wardrobe of) in real life. It's the reason Jen is still starring in hit movies and on the cover of magazines all these years later.

-BUFFAY-TRIBBIANI CUP

WINNER!

Matthew Perry

BEST DELIVERY OF A WITHERING ONE-LINER

Matt wasn't just the beast of great put-downs, he was the much needed voice of reason in a sea of Phoebe and Joey. Matthew Perry made us try harder to be funnier, to be quicker and smarter. Fashion inspo – not so much.

WINNER!

David Schwimmer

BEST PHYSICAL COMEDIAN

This man makes us laugh before uttering a single line. He knows when to take it to 10 and when to subtly pull it back. David Schwimmer was a master at being both desperate and the buffoon, but somehow still managed to break our hearts.

WINNER!

Lisa Kudrow

BEST DISPLAY OF HUMANITY

On paper Phoebe is a ridiculous joke, on-screen she's a living, breathing party-of-one, who feels bizarrely believable. Lisa Kudrow takes us to crazy, but finds something real in Phoebe who is always true to herself and deserves our full respect.

95

CREDITS